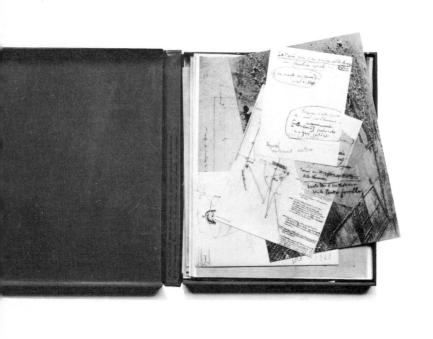

THE BRIDE STRIPPED BARE BY HER BACHELORS, EVEN

**a typographic version by Richard Hamilton
of MARCEL DUCHAMP'S Green Box
translated by George Heard Hamilton**

published by Edition Hansjörg Mayer
Stuttgart, London, Reykjavík

First published 1960 in an edition of 1000 copies
by Percy Lund, Humphries and Co. Ltd, London and Bradford
and George Wittenborn Inc., New York

Second publication 1963 in an edition of 1000 copies
by Percy Lund, Humphries and Co. Ltd, London and Bradford

Third publication 1976 in an edition of 2500 copies
by Edition Hansjörg Mayer, Stuttgart, London, Reykjavík
and Jaap Rietman Inc., New York

Library of Congress Card Catalog Number: 60-13215
Printed in West Germany

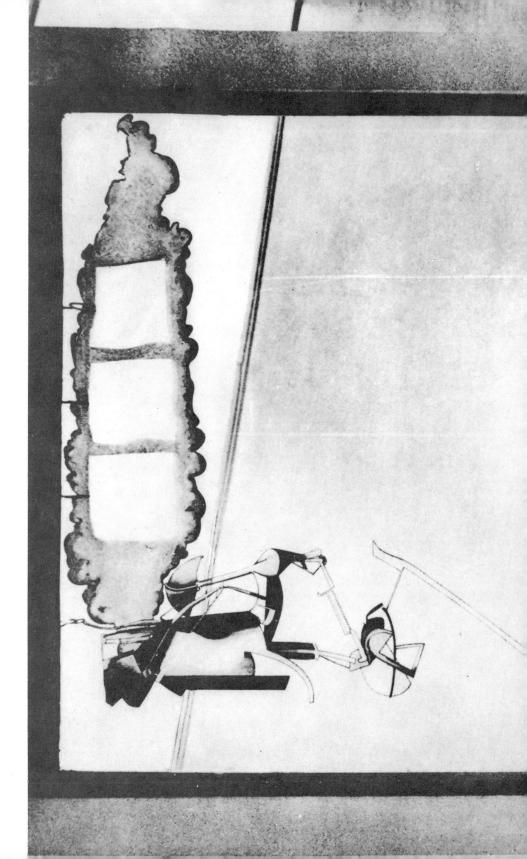

THE BRIDE STRIPPED BARE BY HER BACHELORS, EVEN (Glass—2m.70 high—1915—23)

THE Bride stripped bare by her bachelors

— (Agricultural machine) — even

(a world in yellow)

preferably in the text ?

In reply to your esteemed letter
of the . . . inst. I have the honor . . .

~~M Duchamp 1913.~~
**[this business] has
much to offer . . . .)**
not on the title page –

Apparatus

instrument for farming

Kind of Sub-Title

Delay in Glass

Use "delay" instead of "picture" or
"painting"; "picture on glass" becomes
"delay in glass"—but "delay in
glass" does not mean "picture
on glass"—

    It's merely a way
of succeeding in no longer thinking
that the thing in question is
a picture—to make a "delay" of it
in the most general way possible,
not so much in the different meanings
in which "delay" can be taken, but
rather in their indecisive reunion
"delay"—a "delay in glass"

      as you would say a "poem in prose"

        or a spittoon in silver

Note: This was repunctuated by Marcel Duchamp in February 1957. GHH

Given 1. the waterfall

      2. the illuminating gas,

     one will determine
     we shall (determine) the conditions
                          ?
for the instantaneous State of Rest (or allegorical appearance)

of a (succession) [of a group] of (various facts)

seeming to necessitate each other

under certain laws, in order to isolate the (sign)
  the
of accordance between, on the one hand,
                 all the   (?)
this State of Rest (capable of (innumerable eccentricities)

and, on the other, a choice of Possibilities

authorized by these laws and (also

(determining them.

     For the instantaneous state of rest = bring in

     the term: extra-rapid

We shall determine the conditions of [the] best

exposé of the extra-rapid State of Rest [of the

extra-rapid exposure (= allegorical appearance).

of a group . . . . . . etc.

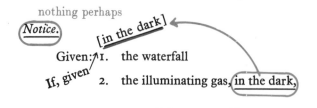

Notice.

[in the dark]

Given: 1.   the waterfall

If, given   2.   the illuminating gas, in the dark,

consider   considerations

we shall determine (the conditions for) the extra-rapid
organization   allegorical Reproduction
exposition (= allegorical appearance) of several

collisions seeming strictly to succeed
[assaults]   unnecessary
each other according to certain laws, in order to
                    the
isolate the Sign of accordance between this

extra-rapid exposition (capable of all the

eccentricities) on the one hand and the choice of the possi-

bilities authorized by these laws on the other.

Algebraic comparison

    a   a being the exposition

    $\dfrac{}{b}$ b „   the possibilities

the ratio $\dfrac{a}{b}$ is in no way given by a

                   (-)
number c $\dfrac{a}{b}$ =c but by the sign which separates

          as soon as   are
a and b; a and b   being " known,, they become

new   relative
units and lose their numerical value (or in duration);

      of ratio
; the sign ⤿/which separated them remains (sign of the

                      ?
accordance or rather of . . . . . . look for it)

1 *1912*

The machine with 5 hearts, the pure
child of nickel and platinum must
dominate the Jura-Paris road.

On the one hand, the chief of the 5 nudes will be
ahead of the 4 other nudes (towards) this
Jura-Paris road. On the other hand, the headlight
child will be the instrument conquering
this Jura-Paris road

This headlight child could, graphically,
be a comet, which would have its
tail in front, this tail being an
appendage of the headlight child
appendage which absorbs by
crushing (gold dust, graphically)
this Jura-Paris road.

The Jura-Paris road, having
to be infinite only humanly,
will lose none of its character of infinity
in finding a termination at one end
in the chief of the 5 nudes, at the other
in the headlight child.

more

The term "indefinite,, seems to me accurate
than infinite. The road will begin
in the chief of the 5 nudes. and will not

end in the headlight child.   2

   Graphically, this road

will tend towards the pure geometrical line

without thickness (the meeting of 2 planes

seems to me the only pictorial means to achieve

purity)

   But in the beginning (in

the chief of the 5 nudes) it will be very finite in

width, thickness ^{etc}, in order little by little,

to become without topographical form in

coming close to this ideal straight line which

finds its opening towards the infinite in the headlight

child.

The pictorial matter of this Jura-Paris road

will be <u>wood</u> which seems to me like

the affective translation of powdered silex.

   Perhaps, see if it is necessary to

choose an essence of wood. (the fir tree,

or then polished mahogany)

————————————————

Details of execution.

Dimensions.—Plans.

Size of the canvas.

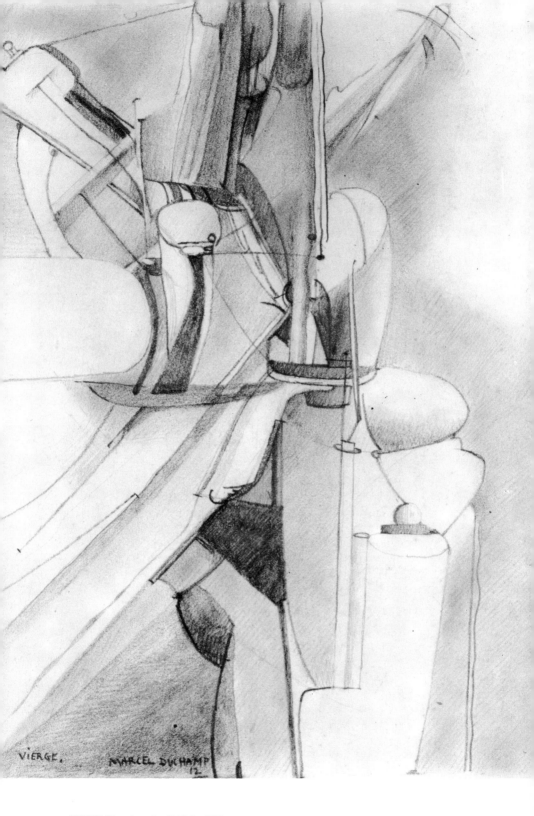

VIRGIN (Drawing—0m.40 high—1912)

The Bride.   skeleton.

        The Bride, at her base, is a reservoir of
love gasoline. (or timid-power). This
timid-power, distributed to the motor with

quite feeble cylinders, in contact with the sparks [II]
of her constant life (desire-magneto) explodes
and makes this virgin blossom who has
attained her desire.

Besides the sparks of the desire-magneto, the
artificial sparks which are produced by the
electrical stripping should supply
explosions in the motor with quite feeble
cylinders.

Hence, this motor with quite feeble cylinders has
2 strokes. The 1st stroke (sparks of the
desire-magneto) controls the immobile
arbor-type. This arbor-type is a
kind of spinal column and should be
the support for the blossoming into
the bride's voluntary stripping.
The 2nd stroke (artificial sparks of
the electrical stripping) controls
the clockwork machinery, graphic translation
of the blossoming into stripping
by the bachelors. (expressing the
throbbing jerk of the minute hand
on electric clocks.)

The Bride accepts this stripping
by the bachelors, since she supplies
the love gasoline to the sparks of this
electrical stripping; moreover, she
furthers her complete nudity by adding to
the 1st focus of sparks (electrical stripping)
the 2nd focus of sparks of the desire-magneto.

<u>Blossoming.</u>

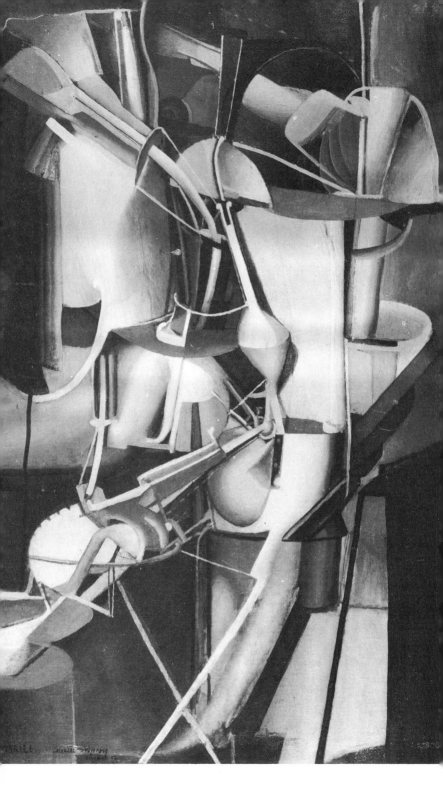

BRIDE (Oil—0m.90 high—1912)

the Bride stripped bare by the bachelors

2 principal elements: 1. Bride
                      2. Bachelors

Graphic arrangement.
a long canvas, upright.
Bride above—
bachelors below.

The bachelors serving as an
architectonic base for the Bride
the latter becomes a sort of
apotheosis of virginity.

— Steam engine
on a masonry substructure
on this brick base. a solid foundation,
the Bachelor-Machine fat
lubricious—(to develop.)
    At the place (still ascending)
where this eroticism is revealed (which should
be one of the principal cogs in the
    Bachelor Machine.
       tormented   2
This gearing gives birth
to the desire-part of the machine
This desire-part—then alters
its mechanical state—which from
steam passes to the state of
internal combustion engine.
(Develop the desire motor,
consequence of the lubricous gearing.)

This desire motor is the last
part of the Bachelor Machine.
Far from being in direct
contact with the Bride. the desire
motor is separated by an air
cooler. (or water).
    This cooler. (graphically)
to express the fact that the
Bride, instead of being merely
an a-sensual icicle, warmly
rejects. (not chastely)

the bachelors' brusque offer this cooler
will be in transparent glass. Several plates
of glass one above the other.,

3

In spite of this cooler.
there is no discontinuity
between the Bachelor Machine and the Bride.
But the connections. will be. <u>electrical</u> and will thus
express the stripping: an alternating process.
Short circuit if necessary.

Bride

Plate of glass

Take care of the fastening: it is necessary to <u>stress</u>
the introduction of the new motor: the Bride.

bach.

<u>Bride</u>. In general, if this bride motor must
appear as an apotheosis of virginity. i.e.
ignorant desire. blank desire. (with a touch
of malice) and if it (graphically) does not
need to satisfy the laws of weighted balance
nonetheless. a shiny metal gallows
could simulate the maiden's attachment to her girl friends
and relatives. (the former and the latter corresponding graphically
to a solid base. on firm ground, like
the masonry base of the bachelor machine
which also rests on firm ground
   basically

4

The Bride is a motor. But
before being a motor which transmits her
timid-power—she is this very timid-
power—This timid-power
is a sort of automobiline, love gasoline
that, distributed to the quite feeble cylinders,
within reach of the <u>sparks of her constant</u>
<u>life,</u> is used for the blossoming
of this virgin who has reached the goal of her desire.
(Here the desire-gears will occupy less space
than in the Bachelor Machine.—They are only
the string that binds the bouquet.)
The whole graphic significance is
for this cinematic blossoming.

This cinematic blossoming is controlled
by the electrical stripping (See the passage of the
Bachelor Machine to the Bride)

3rd Blossoming-crown (Composed
　　　of the 2 preceding).
　　　the 1st blossoming is attached
　　　to the motor with quite feeble cylinders.
　　　The 2nd to the arbor-type, of which it is the
　　　cinematic development.
　　　　The arbor-type has its roots in the desire-
　　　gear, a constituent, skeletal part
　　　of the Bride.
　　　　The motor with quite feeble cylinders
　　　is a superficial organ of the Bride; it is activated
　　　by the love gasoline, a secretion of the
　　　Bride's sexual glands and by the electric
　　　　　　　　sparks of the stripping.
　　　(to show that the Bride does not refuse
　　　this stripping by the bachelors, even
　　　accepts it since she furnishes the love gasoline
　　　and goes so far as to help towards complete nudity
　　　by developing in a sparkling fashion
　　　her intense desire for the orgasm.

　　　Thus the motor with quite feeble cylinders a
　　　constituent but superficial organ of the Bride, is
the 2 foci of the blossoming
　　　　　　ellipse. (the 1st focus the center of
　　　　　　the blossoming into stripping by the bachelors.
　　　　　　2nd focus, center of the voluntarily
　　　　　　imagined blossoming of the Bride.
　　　　　　2nd focus, actuating the desire gears
　　　　　　(the skeletal part of the Bride) giving
　　　　　　birth to the arbor-type etc.

Develop graphically
Thus 1st the blossoming into the stripping
   by the bachelors.
      2nd the blossoming. into the imaginative
   stripping by the Bride-desiring.

      3rd From the 2 graphic developments obtained
find their conciliation. which should be the "blossoming,,
   without causal distinction.
      Mixture, physical compound of the
   2. causes (bachelors and imaginative desire)
unanalysable by logic.
      The last state of this nude
   bride before the orgasm which
   may (might) bring about her fall
      graphically, the need to express,
in a completely different way from the
rest of the painting, this blossoming.

   1st <u>Blossoming into the stripping by bachelors.</u>
Electrical control
      This blossoming-effect of the electrical stripping
should, graphically, end in the clockwork
movement (electric clocks in railway stations)
Gearwheels, cogs, etc (develop
expressing indeed the throbbing jerk of the
minute hand.
      The whole in matt metal. (fine copper, steel
silver,

   2nd Blossoming as stripping voluntarily
imagined by the Bride-desiring.
      This blossoming should be the refined
development of the arbor-type.
      It is born as boughs on
this arbor-type.
      Boughs frosted in nickel and platinum.
As it gradually leaves the arbor, this blossoming
is the image of a motor car climbing a
slope in low gear. (The car wants more
and more to reach the top, and while
slowly accelerating, as if exhausted by hope,
the motor of the car turns over
faster and faster, until it roars
triumphantly.

This cinematic blossoming which expresses
the moment of the stripping, should be grafted on
to an arbor-type of the Bride. This arbor-type
has its roots in the desire-gears. But the cinematic
effects of the electrical stripping, transmitted
to the motor with quite feeble
cylinders, leave (plastic necessity) the
arbor-type at rest—(graphically, in Munich I had already
made 2 studies of this arbor-type)
and do not touch. the desire-gears which
by giving birth to the arbor-type, find
within this arbor-type
the transmission of the desire to the blossoming
into stripping voluntarily imagined by the Bride desiring.

This electrical stripping. sets in motion the
motor with quite feeble cylinders which reveals
the blossoming into stripping by the bachelors
in its action on the clockwork gears.

Grafting itself on the arbor-type—the cinematic
blossoming (controlled by the electrical stripping)
this cinematic blossoming is the
most important part of the painting. (
graphically as a surface)
    It is, in general, the halo of the
Bride, the sum total
of her splendid vibrations: graphically,
there is no question of symbolizing by
a grandiose painting this happy
goal—the Bride's desire; only
more clearly, in all this blossoming,
the painting will be an inventory of the elements
of this blossoming, elements of
the sexual life imagined by her the bride-desiring.
In this blossoming,
The Bride reveals herself nude
in 2 appearances: the first, that of
the stripping by the bachelors. the second
appearance that voluntary-imaginative
one of the Bride. On the coupling of
these 2 appearances of pure virginity—
On their collision, depends the whole
blossoming, the upper part
and crown of the picture.

Sex Cylinder –
(Wasp).

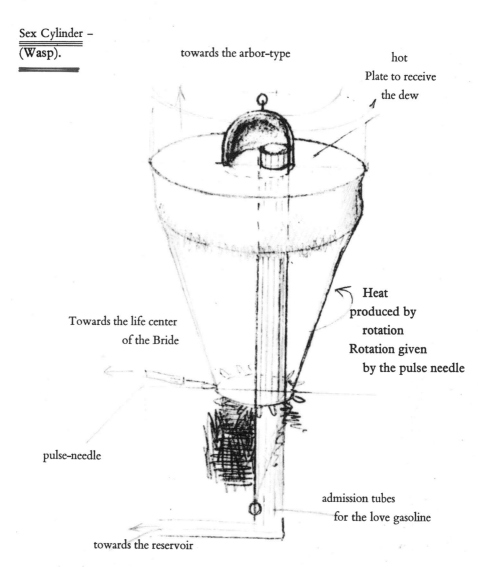

towards the arbor-type

hot
Plate to receive
the dew

Towards the life center
of the Bride

Heat
produced by
rotation
Rotation given
by the pulse needle

pulse-needle

admission tubes
for the love gasoline

towards the reservoir

Ventilation: Start from an interior
draft –

the pulse needle should have its source in **the life center.** of the
Bride. (The Bride has a life center—**the bachelors** have
not. They live on coal or other raw **material**
drawn not from them but from their not them.

The pulse needle in addition to its vibratory movement is
mounted on a wandering leash. It has
the liberty of caged animals—on condition that it
will provide (by its vibratory movement actuating the
sex cylinder) the ventilation on the pole
[at the drum]. This pulse needle will thus promenade
in balance the sex cylinder which spits
at the drum the dew which is to nourish the
vessels of the filament paste and at the
same time imparts to the Pendu its
swinging in relation to the 4 cardinal points.

Wasp=
      Properties:

            1st Secretion of love gasoline by
            osmosis

            2nd Flair or the sense which receives the waves
            of unbalance from the black ball
            In relation to the Pendu's
            upper part (which distributes the
            orders of new balance to
            each of the poles.)

            3rd Vibratory property determining
            the pulsations of the needle.

            4th Ventilation. determining
            the swinging (to and)
            (fro) of the Pendu with its
            accessories.

Reservoir - - -
concerning the
nourishment layer
of the wasp.
    The reservoir will end at the bottom with a
liquid layer from which the sex wasp will take
the necessary dose to sprinkle the drum and
to nourish the filament substance. This liquid
layer will be contained in the oscillating bathtub
(hygiene of the Bride.)

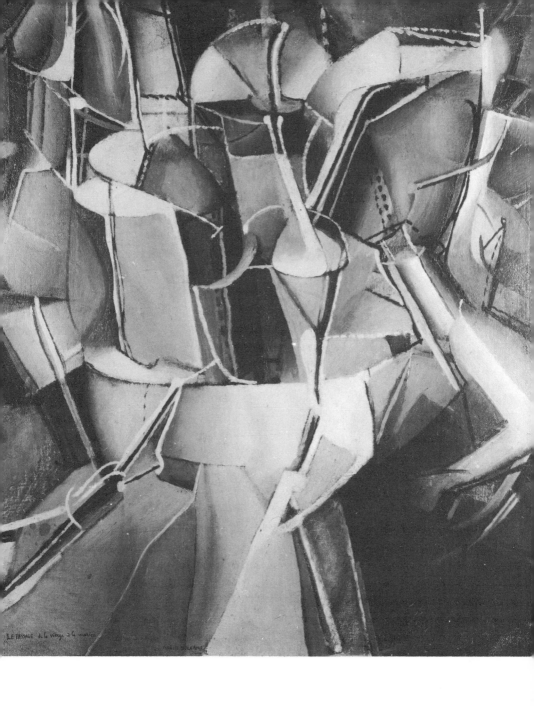

PASSAGE OF THE VIRGIN TO THE BRIDE (Oil—0m.55 high—1912)

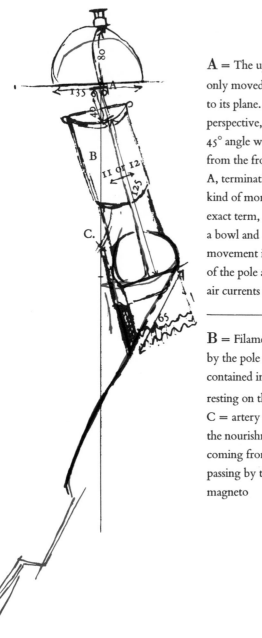

A = The upper part remains fixed and is only moved in a plane parallll to its plane. [In perspective, vertical plane at a 45° angle with a vertical plane seen from the front (35° or 40° perhaps)] At A, terminating the pole a kind of mortice (look for the exact term, held by a bowl and permitting movement in all directions of the pole agitated by the air currents

This angle will express the necessary and sufficient twinkle of the eye.

B = Filament substance carried by the pole (behind) and contained in an open frame

(?)

resting on the magneto –

C = artery channeling the nourishment of the filament substance, coming from the sex wasp (?) while passing by the desire regulator (desire magneto

1913

In the Pendu femelle—and the blossoming

Barometer.

The filament substance might
lengthen or shorten itself in response to an
atmospheric pressure organized
by the wasp. (Filament substance
extremely sensitive to
differences of artificial
atmospheric pressure controlled by the
wasp).

— Isolated cage — *Containing*
the filament
substance
in which would take place —

the storms and the

fine weathers of the wasp.

the filament substance in its meteorological extension
(part relating the pendu
to the handler)
resembles a solid flame, i.e. having a solid
force. It licks the ball of the handler
displacing it
as it pleases

The Pendu femelle
  is the form
  in <u>ordinary perspective</u>
of a Pendu femelle
for which one could perhaps
try to discover
the true form

————————

This comes from the
fact that any
form is the perspective
of another form
according to a certain <u>vanishing point</u>
and a certain <u>distance</u>

Perhaps make
a <u>hinge</u>
<u>picture.</u>
(folding yardstick, book . . . .)
develop
the <u>principle of the hinge</u>
in the displacements
1st in the plane 2nd in space

find an <u>automatic description</u>
of the hinge

---

perhaps introduce it
in the Pendu femelle

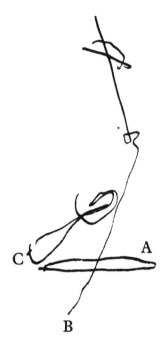

C   A

B

B and C (as they sway.)
just. strike the
circle A.   B below, C
above—The above and the below.
should be used in the decisions
or inscriptions transmitted through
the draft pistons.

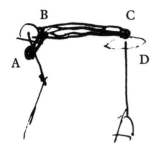

B   C

A   D

[Blossoming] ABC . .

To make an Inscription of it (title,).

       Moving inscription.   i.e. in which the group

of alphabetic units should no longer have a strict order

from left to right—each alphabetic unit will be
         only
present once in the group A B C.

and will be displaced from A to C and back again.

     ——— Since, from A towards C, the inscription should, according

to the need for equilibrium of the plate D, displace

a [stabiliser] (a ball or anything). On this plate D.

At A. there will be [a sort of letter box] (alphabet)

which will go towards B and C. (to develop and study)

Representation of this inscription: Photographic method
Determine   their
~~Establish~~ the alphabetic units (number, form,

significance . .).

represent sculpturally this inscription

in movement.

  and take a snapshot. have it enlarged

to the final dimensions.—With the negative

of the enlargement : have prepared with silver

bromide—the large plate glass and make a

print. directly. on the back. (ask

a photographer for information—).

    Perhaps look for a way to obtain

superimposed prints—i.e. a first

               alphabetic
print—of the first unit (for instance)

hyposulphite.—make a second print

of the second alphabetic unit superimposing

itself on the first but printing only the essential

without a background (the transparent background of the glass)

3rd 4th 5th etc. units.

    all that to be studied for the execution.

(Perhaps have a <u>half-tone block</u>

made. simply to print.).

      ? ? ?

Perhaps use

    a less transparent (ground glass
            or varnish
or oiled paper on the glass) allowing

a provisional opacity made by the

splashes from upstream and down.

[for the top ''Inscription,,].
     blossoming.

1914

Kind of milky
way flesh color
surrounding
unevenly densely
the 3 Pistons (i.e.
there will be a transparent
layer on
the glass then the 3 Pistons
then another layer
of milky way)
This flesh-like milky way
to be used as a

support for the inscription

which is concerned with

the cannon shots (at A)

<u>Top inscription.</u>

obtained with the

draft pistons.

(indicate the way

to "prepare" these

pistons.).

Then "place" them for
(2 to 3 months)
a certain time. and let

them leave their

imprint as

3 <u>nets</u> through which

pass the commands

of the Pendu femelle (commands

having their alphabet and

terms governed by the

orientation of the 3 nets

[a sort of triple "<u>cipher</u>"

through which

the milky way supports

and guides

the said commands]

Next remove them

so that nothing remains

but their firm

imprint i.e. the

<u>form</u> permitting all

combinations of letters sent
across
commands, orders   this said triple
form,
authorizations, etc

which must

join the shots

and the splash

Use a radiator and

a piece of paper (or something else)

moved by the heat

above.

      photo. 3. performances—

probably with a background

giving

a better indication of the

displacements and deformations.

———————

(perhaps use that for the splash)

↘ 3 Photos of a piece of white cloth—

piston of the draft; i . e .

cloth accepted and rejected

    by the draft.

    (To avoid any play of light, make
            on the cloth flat before the photo
    symmetrical marks, in the form of points or

    small squares equal and at equal distances

    from each other [perhaps cut out]; after

    the photo, the group of marked squares

disSymmetrically arranged, will present

    on a flat surface a conventional representation

    of the 3 draft pistons.

May.

1915.

Shots.

From more or less far; on a <u>target</u>.

This target in short <u>corresponds</u>

to the vanishing point (in perspective.)

The figure thus obtained will be the

projection (<u>through skill</u>) of the principal

points of a 3 dimensional body.—With

maximum skill, this projection would

be reduced to a point (the target).

With ordinary skill this

projection will be a demultiplication

of the target. (Each of the new points

[images of the target] will have a

coefficient of displacement. This coefficient

is nothing but a souvenir and can be noted

conventionally (The different shots

tinted from black to white according to their

distance)—

In general, the figure obtained

is the <u>visible</u> flattening (a stop

on the way) of the demultiplied

body

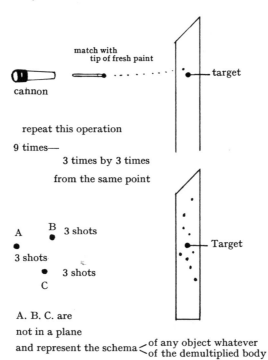

match with
tip of fresh paint

cannon

— target

repeat this operation

9 times—

3 times by 3 times

from the same point

A   B   3 shots

3 shots

3 shots

C

— Target

A. B. C. are

not in a plane

and represent the schema $<$ of any object whatever
of the demultiplied body

Wind—for the draft pistons
Skill—for the holes
Weight—for the standard-stops

    to be developed—

The principal forms of the Bachelor Machine
are imperfect: rectangle, circle, parallelepiped,
symmetrical handle, demi-sphere = i.e.
they are mensurable (relation of their
dimensions among themselves. and relation of these
principal forms
to their destination in the Bachelor Machine)
In the Bride, the principal forms
are more or
less large or small, have no
longer, in relation to their destination
a mensurability: a sphere, in
the Bride will be of some radius or other
(the radius given in the representation
is fictitious and dotted.)
    Similarly and better in the Pendu
femelle and the [Wasp] , parabolas
hyperbolas (or volumes deriving
from them) will lose all character
of mensurable position.
The actual representation will be
but one example of each of these
principal freed forms. (An
example without representational value, but
permitting the more or less).

<u>Waterfall.</u>

A sort of waterspout coming

from a distance in a half circle

over the malic moulds

(seen from the side)

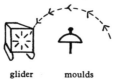

glider   moulds

Water mill (landscape—).

Given the waterfall

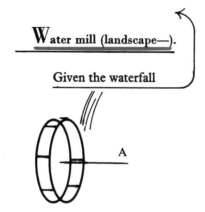

A

Draw it full size—

A ≡ <u>axis</u> of the wheel <u>which</u> should drag the bottle of Benedictine.
the bottles

Speed of the mill wheel

Hook

falling from the top of the bachelor apparatus

take a hook—

considerably enlarged.

and functioning in the basement—which
                          placed
it enters through 2 holes between

the glider and the grinder

Hook

(from below)

At the top of the glass ⁼ a sort of fork

[heavier going down than

coming up (so as to save the power

of the waterfall)] must fall

astride the axle going

from the glider to the grinder.

This fork is high enough

 not to touch this

(this fork will be an
ordinary hook considerably
enlarged)

axle and the two points of

the fork

will penetrate into the basement

through two holes. In this basement

it actuates the glider by its

fall It makes it come

towards the grinder. and at the same

time opens the scissors.

p.t.o.

to the top
It rises again by means of the

chain engaged on the axle of the

water mill. which turns
with (**A**
a sprocket   an increased gear ratio

so that it goes faster.

B fork .

B   **A**

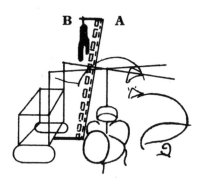

the Hook which falls between Grinder

and Glider and which

makes the glider glide,

Is made of a substance

of oscillating density. This

hook therefore has an indeterminate,

variable, and uncontrollable

weight.—It is by

this oscillating density that

the choice is made between the 3 crashes:
strength of the
according to the fall of the hook

the decelerations or accelerations

(caused by the continual changes

of density,) the right is

chosen rather than the left

or alternatively or the centre.

[More simply]:

the glider goes and comes.

It goes: a (weight) falls

and makes it go

It comes:

By friction

of the runners the metal of the glider

responds elastically

a little

i.e. the glider resumes more slowly

its first position, as it sends back

in the air

the (weight) . ŭnd so weiter.

By condescension, this

weight is denser going

down than going up

[find a concrete object which could

respond to this changing

density]

WATER MILL WITHIN GLIDER (Glass—1m. high—1913–15)

~~Chariot.~~   Sleigh —   Glider

the litanies of the Chariot:
~~Slow life.~~
Vicious circle.
Onanism.
Horizontal.
Round trip
for the buffer.
Junk of life.
Cheap construction.
Tin, cords,
iron wire.
Eccentric wooden
pulleys.
Monotonous fly wheel.
Beer professor.
(to be entirely redone).

      •

draw the
scheme of the •
chariot

~~The Chariot should be made of rods~~

~~of emancipated metal; the chariot~~

~~would have the property of giving itself~~
without resistance of gravity
~~to a force acting horizontally~~

~~upon it.~~ (See the fall of the weight, in

the form of a bottle of Benedictine) •

The sleigh mounted on runners

dovetailed into an underground rail,

after having been drawn from A to B. returns

to its 1st position by the phenomenon of inversion

of friction. The friction

of the runner on the rail [instead of

changing into heat] is transformed

into a returning force equal to the going force.

(This phenomenon in relation to the emancipa-

tion of the metal which forms the body

of the rods of the ~~chariot.~~ sleigh

A   B

Principle: +

friction
reintegrated

Chariot — Sleigh — Glider

Exposé of the Chariot (in the text = litanies of the chariot)

— Slow life —

— Vicious circle —

— Onanism —

— Horizontal —

— Buffer of life —

— Bachelor life regarded as an alternating rebounding on this buffer.

— Rebounding = junk of life

— Cheap construction

— Tin

— Cords

— Iron wire

— Crude wooden pulleys

— Eccentrics

— Monotonous fly wheel

Buffer of life = stopping the action not by

brutal opposition but by

extended springs slowly resuming

their first position.

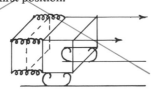

The metal (or material)—of the chariot is
emancipated. i.e.: that it has a weight
but a force acting horizontally
on the chariot does not have to support this
weight (the weight of the metal does not impede
a horizontal traction (to be developed)). The
chariot is emancipated horizontally. it is
free of all gravity in the horizontal

plane (property of the metal of the rods of which
the chariot is made)

These rods are of this shape: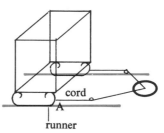

square section

1 cm section
across the center (size
apparent
on the
final version

ordinary type.

color: yellow green. (like the queen in the

King and Queen . . . .)

See also: for this color the Munich notes
on the composition of the colors in the first studies

(Light cadmium
and white)

The chariot is supported by runners which
slide (oil etc.) in a groove

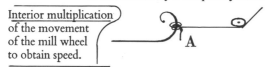

cord

A

runner

the cord, which has to pull the chariot under
the blow of the bottle weight, is attached at A
to the runner by a temporary knot.

Interior multiplication
of the movement
of the mill wheel
to obtain speed.

A

Projection of the chariot

length = to the drop of the bottle
weight
at O

cord

O

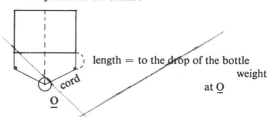

Behind (at the left of the picture) the chariot is brought back into position
by the Sandow.   In the picture the sandows will be
at rest (almost relaxed)

Sandow

Note: *Sandow*, in French a mechanical chest-expander, so-called after the famous strong
man. GHH

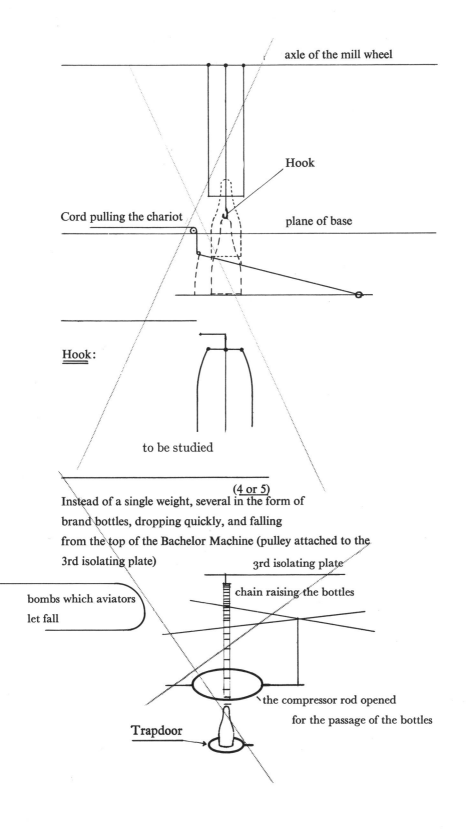

axle of the mill wheel

Hook

Cord pulling the chariot

plane of base

Hook:

to be studied

(4 or 5)
Instead of a single weight, several in the form of
brand bottles, dropping quickly, and falling
from the top of the Bachelor Machine (pulley attached to the
3rd isolating plate)

3rd isolating plate

bombs which aviators
let fall

chain raising the bottles

the compressor rod opened

for the passage of the bottles

Trapdoor

Bottle of Benedictine
as a form of the Weight.

4 Weights in the form of

Brand bottles

fig.

The chariot should, while reciting its litanies, go from

A to B. and return from B to A. at a

jerky pace., it appears in the costume of Eman-

cipation, hiding in its bosom the landscape of the water

paragraph

mill, it necessarily follows that a lead weight

?

to the 3rd power in the form of a bottle of Benedictine

acting normally on a system of

cords attached to the chariot, would force it to

come from A to B.   much too far-fetched

   The springs x and x′ . . . . restore it immediately afterwards to

its initial position (A).

of the revolution
of the bottle
of Benedictine.

Song :—After having pulled the chariot by its fall,

the bottle of Benedictine lets itself

fig. C

be raised by the hook; it falls asleep as

it goes up., the dead point wakes it up

suddenly and with its head down. It pirouettes and,

falls vertically

according to the laws of gravity.

   or (Body)   with lead bottoms
Molecular composition of the bottles, such that it is impossible to
calculate their weight. = Great density and in perpetual movement
not at all fixed like that of metals (oscillating density). It is by
this oscillating density that the choice is made between the 3 crashes
It is truly this oscillating density that expresses the liberty of indifference

Laws, principles, phenomena

— Phen. of stretching in the unit of length —

— Adage of spontaneity = The bachelor grinds his chocolate himself

— Phen. or principle of oscillating density, a property of the substance of brand bottles.

— { Emancipated metal of the rods of the sleigh

— { Friction re-integrated in reverse (emancipated metal)

the Chocolate Grinder
                              is essentially composed . . .

The chocolate of the rollers, coming from one knows not where,
would deposit itself after grinding, as milk chocolate . . . . .

                 (insert a letter referring to a diagram) with brilliant shimmering
The necktie would have been of aluminum foil stretched and
stuck down, but the³ rollers always turn beneath.

the Bayonet—⁽ˣ⁾Helps to hold up the compression bar
and the large scissors and the isolating plates.

            First-class article.

The grinder is mounted on a Louis XV nickeled
chassis.

        reconsider it
   Adage
Principle of [Spontaneity]   (which explains the gyratory mt of the grinder without other help)
The bachelor grinds his chocolate himself—

   commercial formula, trade mark, commercial slogan

   inscribed like an advertisement on a bit of glossy and

   colored paper (have it made by a printer)—this paper stuck

   on the article "Chocolate Grinder"

The necktie will owe its elegance to its thickness—

$\frac{1}{2}$ cm. or $1^{\underline{cm}}$ at the most
<u>resplendent</u>
It will be brilliant <u>above.</u>

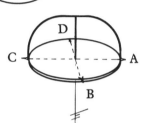

perhaps 4 points on the sides, A B C D.

<u>very pointed (like all neckties)</u>

[to be put in the text]

Description of the necktie:

    1. resplendent in color

    2. provided at the 4 corners with
          very sharp points (like all
neckties.

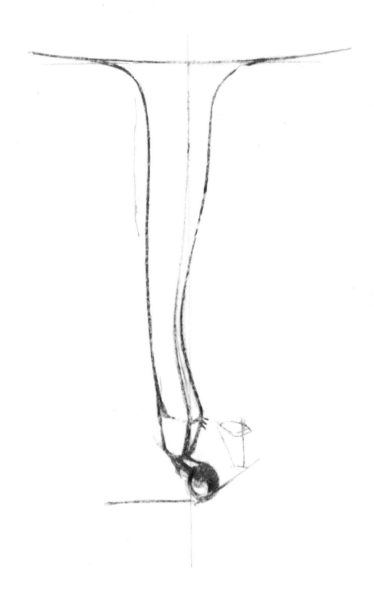

THE LOUIS XV LEG (actual size)

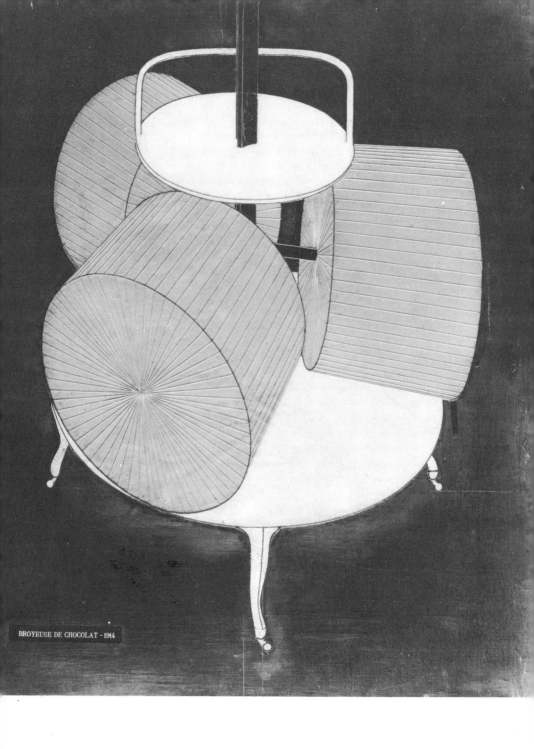

BROYEUSE DE CHOCOLAT - 1914

CHOCOLATE GRINDER (Oil—0m.55 high—1914)

Given an object in chocolate.

1st its appearance = retinal impression (and other sensory consequences)

2nd its apparition

The mould of a chocolate object is the negative apparition [in negative]
of the surface
of the plane (with several curvatures) generating 1st (by one or

elementary prllllism) the colored form of the object

2nd. the mass of elements of light (chocolate type [native colors]

+
in the conditional
tense. if one . . . elements): + in the passage from the apparition (mould) to the appear-

ance, the plane, composed of elements of chocolate type light

determines the apparent chocolate mass

by physical dyeing

a)   in negative   for the colored form
   the negative apparition (determined conventionally by the

linear perspective, but always in an environment
                          (for example)
of n—1 dimensions. for an object of n dimensions.); In the
          in negative
same way this negative apparition, for

the phenomenon of Physical Dyeing, is determined by

the source of light becoming in the apparent object

lighted mass (native colors. = apparition in negative of the

apparent colors of the substance of the objects.)

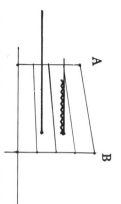

A

B

The whole picture seems to be in papier mâché because the whole of this representation is the sketch (like a mould) for a reality which would be possible by slightly distending the laws of physics and chemistry

Interior lighting.

Instead of an extra-solar light falling at an angle of 45°.

determine the luminous effects (lights and shadows) of an interior source. i.e., that each substance in its chemical composition is endowed with a "phosphorescence,, (?) and lights up like luminous advertisements not quite? Its light is not independent of its color.—In short the color-effect of the whole will be the appearance of matter having a source of light in its molecular construction.

The substance of each part is both a source of light and a color. (in other words the apparent color of each part is the source of visibility in color of that part (with no reflections on the other parts)

Try to find a way to distribute the "distance between molecules". according to the form of each part (roundness, flatness

Begin with darkness (black background) or rather picric yellow)

Strictness of a Huguenot sort.

—Provisional color = The malic forms. They are
provisionally painted with red lead <u>while waiting</u> for each
one to receive its color, like
croquet mallets.

Note: A station-master was added later to complete the nine malic moulds. RH

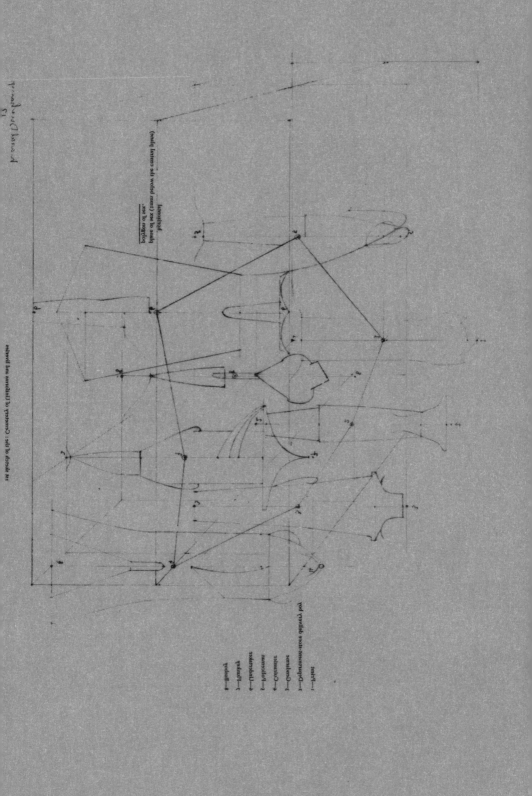

horizontal
plane of sex (1mm below the central plane)
polygon of sex.

Marcel Duchamp
12

1st sketch of the: Cemetery of Uniforms and liveries

1—Priest
2—Department-store delivery boy
3—Gendarme
4—Cuirassier
5—Policeman
6—Undertaker
7—Flunkey
8—Busboy

CEMETERY OF UNIFORMS AND LIVERIES (Drawing—0m.35 long—1913)

Progress (improvement)   Given the illuminating gas.

~~Journey~~ of the illuminating gas up to the planes of flow

Malique moulds. (Malic(?))

By Eros' matrix, we understand the group

of ^{8} uniforms or hollow liveries

       receive the   which takes

destined to give to the illuminating gas 8 malic

forms (gendarme, cuirassier etc.)

The gas castings so obtained

would hear the litanies sung by

the chariot, refrain of the whole celibate machine,

but they will never be able to pass beyond the Mask $=$ They

would have been as if enveloped, alongside their

regrets, by a mirror reflecting back to them their

own complexity to the point of their being hallucinated rather

onanistically. (Cemetery of ^{8} uniforms or liveries)

Each of the 8 malic forms

is built above and below a common

horizontal

plane, the plane of sex cutting them at the point of sex.

(refer to figure)

or   Each of the 8 malic forms is cut by an imaginary
horizontal plane at a point called the point of sex.

Progress (improvement)

~~Journey~~ of the illuminating gas up to the planes of flow. (continued)
24

the capillary tubes

A

each malic form terminates at the head in

3 capillary tubes, the 24 therefore were supposed

to cut the gas in bits and would have led it

to disguise itself as 24 fine

solid needles so that they will become when reunited
2
once again, in the demi-siphons, a fog

made of a thousand spangles of frosty gas.

B

At the head, [at the summit], of each malic mould

3 capillary tubes, 24 in all: to cut the gas

in bits, to cut the gas in long needles

already solid, since before becoming an explosive liquid,
solid
it takes the form of a fog of spangles of frosty gas, all

this by the phenomenon of stretching in the unit of length
(refer to figure)

When the 2 demi-siphons (letter in fig.) would have been filled

with the fog of spangles which

are lighter than air, the operation of
began
the liquefaction of the gas through the sieve and the horizontal filter:

each spangle of solid gas strives (in a kind of spangle

derby) to pass the holes of the sieve

with élan, reacting already to the suction of the pump.

—Improvement of the [illuminating] gas to the slopes.—

as a "Commentary" on the section

Slopes. = have a photograph made of: *to have*

the apprentice in the sun

Note: 'To have the apprentice in the sun' is the title of a drawing in the box of 1914. GHH

(I)

The illuminating gas

(malic forms)

after the malic moulds:

From the top of each malic mould.

the gas passes along the unit of length in

a tube of elemental section. and, by

the phenomenon of stretching in the unit of

length the gas finds itself [congealed] solidified

in the form of elemental rods.

   Each of these rods, under the pressure of the

gas in the malic moulds, leaves its tube and

breaks, through fragility, into unequal spangles.

lighter than air. (retail fog)

(graphically: 8 horizontal tubes —

   elemental section

      to be studied

   etc.)

develop
ais relationship
~ one length
~ the change
~ condition of the
ody (illum. gas)
abmitted to
ais unit
~ length.

a the case
~ stretching,
ae unit of length
~ variable
a relation to the
~ction of the tube.
~iven the unit
~f length with an elemental section
ae tubes with a double section
ill have a length twice (Playful Physics)
ae standard of the elemental section. (This to give
~nportance not to the unit of length
~ut to the phenomenon of stretching the gas.)

~xit of the spangles:
            thus   each
      The gas cut in bits, spangle,

retaining in its smallest parts

the malic tint. liberated at the mouth of the tubes,

tends to rise.

            (parasol Trap)
      The spangles are stopped in

~ee
~ote on their ascent by the 1st parasol (sieve.)
~e Trap

   The sieves (6 probably) are semi-spherical

parasols, with holes. [The holes of the sieves

parasols should give in the shape of a globe the figure

of the 8 malic moulds, given schematic. by the 8 summits

(polygon concave plane). by subsidized symmetry].

~rientation of the parasols:

         The 1st is horizontal, and receives the spangles
as they leave the tubes.
If one joins the centers of the parasols with a line
one obtains a half circumference from A to B.

the network of

Standard stops

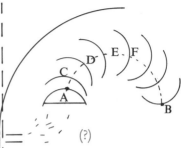

(?)

As in a Derby, the spangles pass through

the parasols A, C D.E F . . . B.

and as they gradually arrive

at D,E,F, . . . etc. they are straightened out

i.e. they lose their sense of up and

down ([more precise term]).—The group

of these parasols forms a

sort of labyrinth of the 3 directions.—

The spangles dazed by this progressive

turning imperceptibly lose [provisionally

they will find it again later] their

designation of left, right, up, down

etc, lose their awareness of

Position

   The parasols. thus straighten out the spangles

which, on leaving the tubes were free

and wished to rise.

   They straighten them out like a

sheet of paper rolled up too much

which one unrolls several times in the

opposite direction.

to the point that: necessarily there is a change

of condition in the spangles. They can no longer

retain their individuality and they all join together

after B.

The illuminating gas (II).   =

A   B

After B.

—Change in the condition of the spangles.—

From their dizziness [provisional],

from their loss of awareness of position,
                                                      through the sieves
   obtained by successive passing and imperceptible change of direction

of these sieves (change of direction of which the terminations are A and B),

   the spangles [dissolve]; the spangles splash themselves each to

itself, i.e. change (little by little through the last sieves)

their condition from: spangles lighter than air, of a certain length, of elemental

thickness with a determination to rise, into: a liquid elemental

scattering, seeking no direction, a scattered Suspension –

  +
snow on their way out at B, Vapor of inertia, but keeping

its liquid character through instinct for cohesion (the only manifestation of

the individuality of the illuminating gas in its habitual games with
(so reduced ! !)
conventional surroundings.

    What a drip!

Ventilator—Churn . (perhaps give it a butterfly form

    sediment of the inert illuminating gas
    in a dense liquid preserving
    the exterior qualities of the dissolved
    spangles—putting up a
    front (before this Ventilator)
    by exaggerating the cohesion.—
    by turning, the ventilator forces
    the gas to attach itself at ab,cd,ef.etc.
    in a condition resembling
    glycerine mixed with water

Pump

to be crossed out

The right and the left are obtained

by letting trail behind you a

tinge of <u>persistence in the situation</u>.

This symmetrical fashioning of the <u>situation</u>

<u>distributed</u> on each side of the vertical axis

is of practical value

(as right different

from left) only as a residue of experiences

on fixed exterior points.

And <u>on the other hand</u>: considered separately

the vertical axis∧ turning on

itself, a generating line at a right

angle e.g. **axis** B will always determine

a circle A in the 2 cases 1st turning

in the direction A, 2nd direction B.—

Thus, <u>if it</u> were still

possible; in the case of the vertical axis at

contrary

rest., to consider 2 <u>directions</u> for

the generating line G., the figure engendered

it

(whatever <u>may</u> be.)

can no longer be called left

or right of the axis—

— As there is gradually less differentiation

from axis to axis., i.e. as all the

axes gradually disappear

in a fading verticality the front and the back,

the reverse and the obverse acquire a

circular significance: the right and

the left which are the 4 arms of the front and

back. melt. <u>along the</u> verticals.

————————————————— (in a fourth dimension)

<u>the interior and exterior</u> can receive

a similar identification. But

the axis is no longer vertical and has no longer

a <u>one</u>-dimensional appearance

COFFEE GRINDER (Cardboard—0m.35 high—1911)

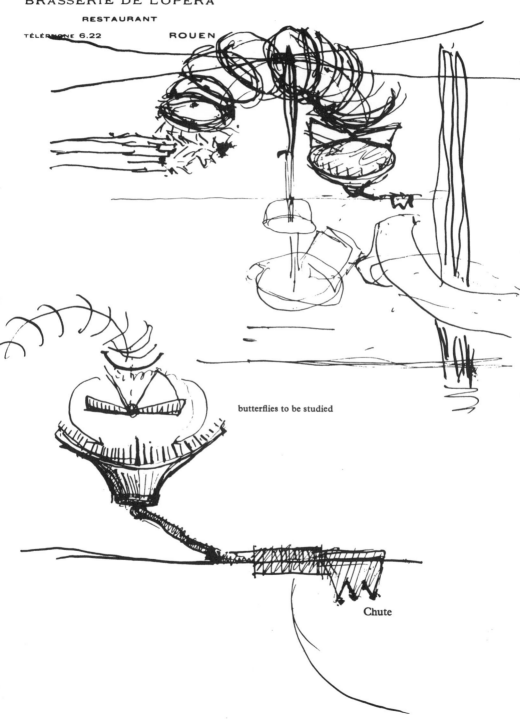

BRASSERIE DE L'OPÉRA

RESTAURANT

TÉLÉPHONE 6.22   ROUEN

butterflies to be studied

Chute

Project— Scale $^1/5$

the figures between parenthesis
indicate the measures $\longrightarrow$ $\dfrac{D}{2} = 14,2,6$ cm
not transposed by the perspective

For the perspective construction
of the intermediate circles A and B:
SR given by division by 3 of the
circumferences. — VT parll to SR .
absoly

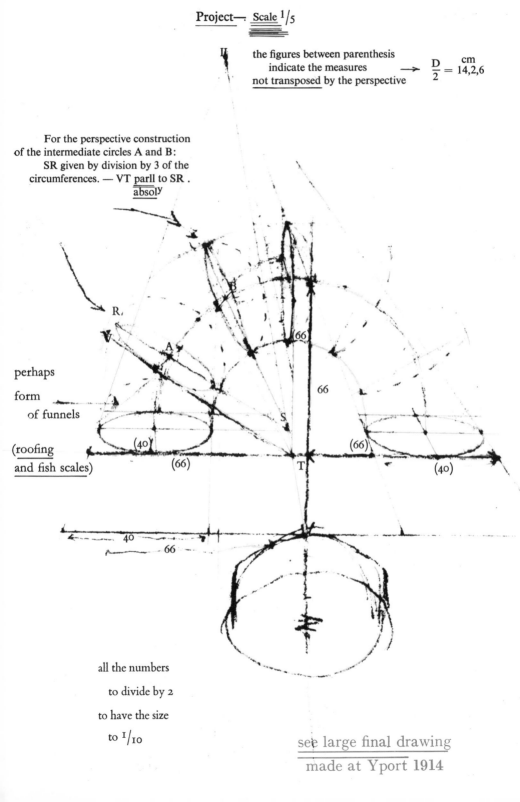

perhaps

form

  of funnels

(roofing

and fish scales)

(40)

(66)

(66)

(40)

66

66

40

66

all the numbers

to divide by 2

to have the size

to $^1/_{10}$

see large final drawing

made at Yport 1914

after the 9 malic forms:

The sieves.

The sieves of the bachelor apparatus are
a reversed image of porosity.

To raise dust

on Dust-Glasses

for 4 months. 6 months. which you

close up afterwards

hermetically. = Transparency

—Differences. To be worked out

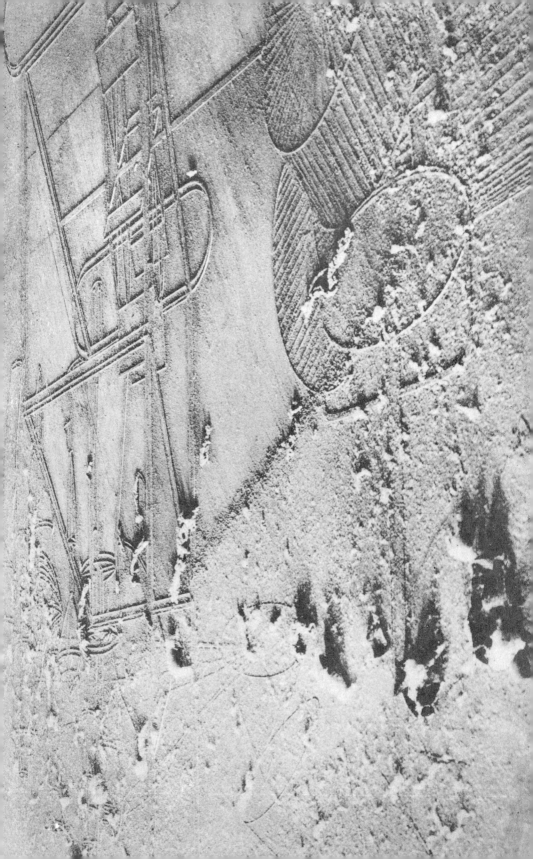

sieves

For the ⌢ in the glass—allow dust to

fall on this part a dust of 3 or 4 months

and wipe well around it in such a way that this dust

will be a kind of color (transparent pastel)

(Use of mica)

To be mentioned the quality of the other side of the dust either as the name of the metal or otherwise

---

Also try to find several layers of transparent colors
(probably with varnish) one above the other. the
whole on glass.——

after the 3 crashes =

Splash. and not
vertical channeling of
the encounter
at the bottom of the slopes.

Study the 3 falls:

    After the center one,

    the(mobile)will splash

    the gas which has become liquid

and arrived at the bottom of the slopes

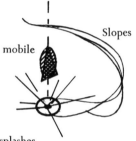

Direct these splashes

    which should be used

for the manoeuvering

    of the handler of gravıty

    (Boxing match.)

GENERAL PLAN—PERSPECTIVE (Drawing—0m.33 high—1914)

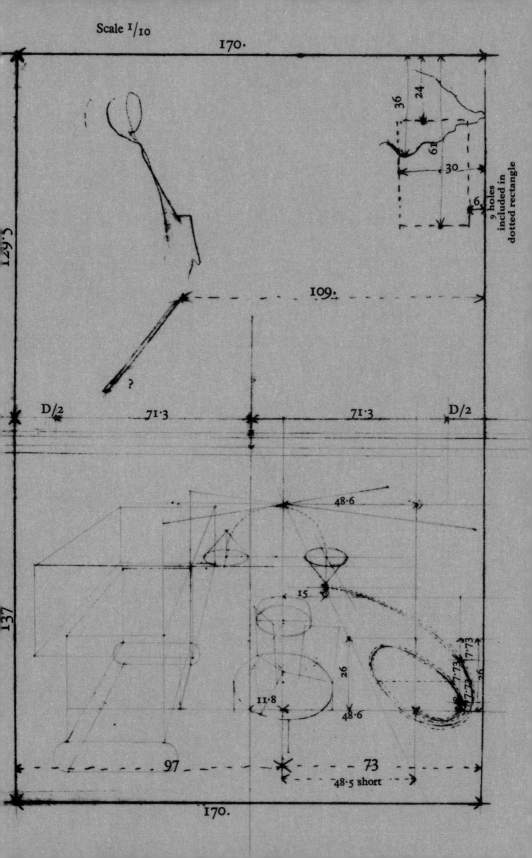

Scale ¹/₁₀

170.

129·5

36

24

61

30

6.

9 holes
included in
dotted rectangle

109.

?

D/2   71·3   71·3   D/2

48·6

15

26

11·8   48·6

137

7·73   7·73

7·73

26

97   73

48·5 short

170.

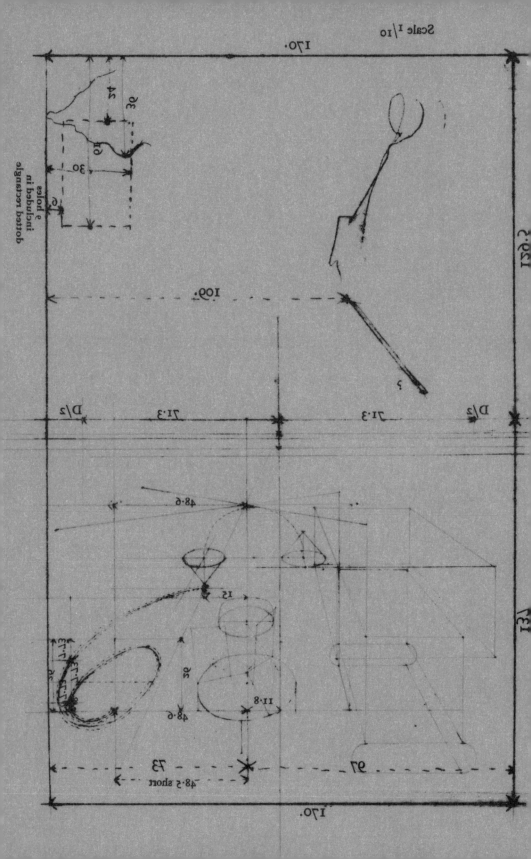

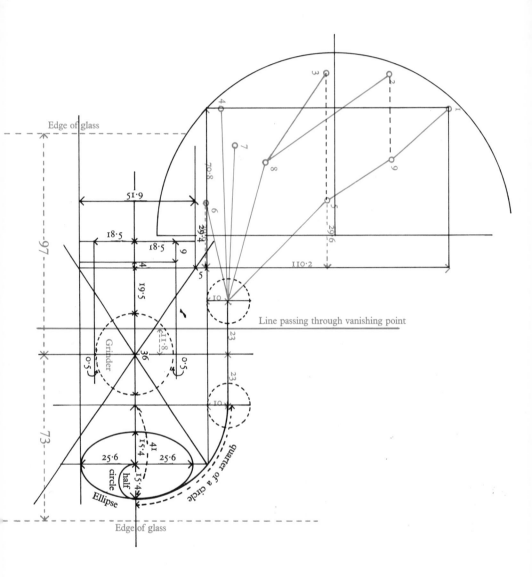

BACHELOR APPARATUS—PLAN (Drawing—0m.30 long—1913)

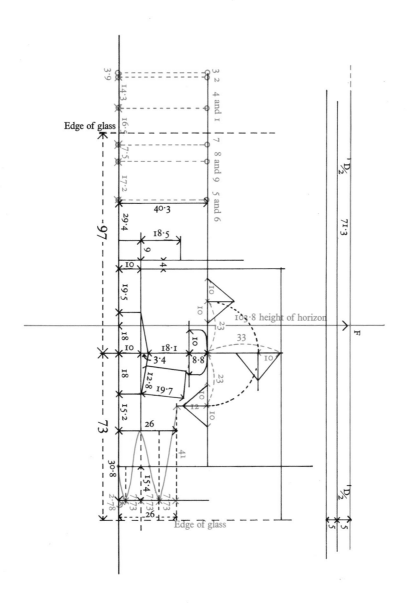

BACHELOR APPARATUS—ELEVATION (Drawing—0m.30 long—1913)

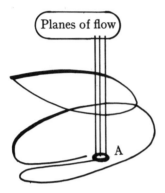

Planes of flow

A

in the form of a toboggan
but more of a corkscrew. and
the splash at A is an uncorking
The group may be described in the sense
of model-uncorking.

The fall to A of the three-crashes helps
the uncorking —

The splash (nothing in common with
champagne) ends the series
of bachelor operations and transforms
the combination of the illuminating gas and the scissors
into a single continuous support, support
which will be regularized by the 9 holes.

OCULIST WITNESSES (Drawing—0m.50 high—1920)

<u>Cones</u>

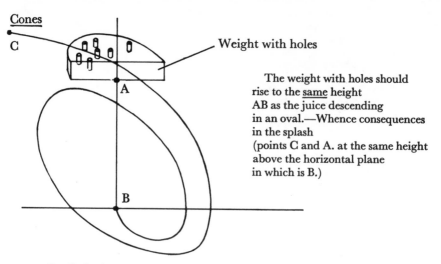

C

A

B

Weight with holes

The weight with holes should
rise to the <u>same</u> height
AB as the juice descending
in an oval.—Whence consequences
in the splash
(points C and A. at the same height
above the horizontal plane
in which is B.)

<u>Oculist's charts</u>—Dazzling of the splash

by the oculist's charts.

Sculpture of drops (points) which the splash forms
after having been dazzled across the
oculist's charts, each drop acting
as a point and sent back mirrorically
to the high part of the glass to meet
the 9 shots =
     Mirrorical return—Each drop
will pass the 3 planes at the horizon
between the perspective and the geometrical drawing of 2 figures which will be
indicated on these 3 planes by the Wilson-Lincoln system (i.e.
like the portraits which seen from the left show
Wilson seen from the right show Lincoln —)

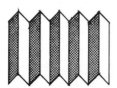

seen from the right the figure may give a square for example
from the front and seen from the right it could give the same
square seen in perspective —
    The mirrorical drops not the drops themselves
but their image pass between these 2 states
of the same figure (square in this example)
    (Perhaps use prisms stuck behind the glass.)
     to obtain the desired effect)

**Note: 'seen from the right' (7th line from the bottom) is my error and should read—seen
from the left. MD 59**

Handler of gravity

[suppress the center]

*make the rod
as a spring (to be studied:*

perhaps —??

Handler
[__TENDer__] of gravity

These 2 terms are complementary.

Note: 'TENDer' is MD's English equivalent for his French 'Soigneur'. RH

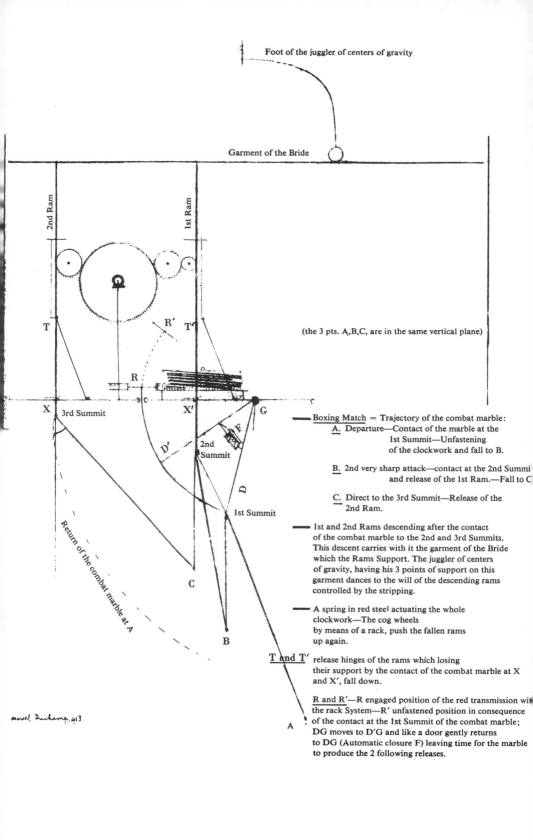

Foot of the juggler of centers of gravity

Garment of the Bride

2nd Ram

1st Ram

T

R′ T′

(the 3 pts. A,B,C, are in the same vertical plane)

R

X 3rd Summit

X′

G

D′ 2nd Summit

F

Return of the combat marble at A

1st Summit

D

C

B

T and T′

R

A

Boxing Match = Trajectory of the combat marble:
A. Departure—Contact of the marble at the
1st Summit—Unfastening
of the clockwork and fall to B.

B. 2nd very sharp attack—contact at the 2nd Summit
and release of the 1st Ram.—Fall to C

C. Direct to the 3rd Summit—Release of the
2nd Ram.

1st and 2nd Rams descending after the contact
of the combat marble to the 2nd and 3rd Summits.
This descent carries with it the garment of the Bride
which the Rams Support. The juggler of centers
of gravity, having his 3 points of support on this
garment dances to the will of the descending rams
controlled by the stripping.

A spring in red steel actuating the whole
clockwork—The cog wheels
by means of a rack, push the fallen rams
up again.

T and T′ release hinges of the rams which losing
their support by the contact of the combat marble at X
and X′, fall down.

R and R′—R engaged position of the red transmission with
the rack System—R′ unfastened position in consequence
of the contact at the 1st Summit of the combat marble;
DG moves to D′G and like a door gently returns
to DG (Automatic closure F) leaving time for the marble
to produce the 2 following releases.

marcel Duchamp, 1913

TO BE LOOKED AT WITH ONE EYE, CLOSE·TO, FOR ALMOST AN HOUR (Glass—0m.45 high—1918)

General notes. for a Hilarious picture.
put the whole Bride under a glass case, or into a transparent
cage.

Contrary to the previous notes, the Bride no longer provides
gasoline for the cylinder-breasts. (Try for a better wording than
"cylinder-breasts")

Of hygiene in the Bride; or of the Diet in the Bride.

give the juggler only 3 feet because 3 points of support are
necessary for stable equilibrium, 2 would give only an
unstable equilibrium

Painting of precision, and beauty of indifference

Solidity of construction:
    Equality of superposition: the principal dimensions
of the general foundation for the Bride and for the Bachelor Machine are
equal.

Directions:
    the form   = space —
    the number 3. taken as a refrain in duration—(number is mathematical
                                                      duration.

Always or nearly always give reasons for the choice between 2 or more
solutions (by ironical causality).

Ironism of affirmation: differences from negative ironism de-
pendent solely on Laughter.

Beer Professor (litany of the chariot)

Principle of subsidized symmetries. (its application in
the movements of the handler
and of the hanged figure; see
the Pendu femelle)

In general, the picture is the apparition
of an appearance (see explanation)

Note: 'Apparition' is to be understood as a lighted appearance from within the picture.
MD 58

Take a Larousse dictionary and copy all the so-called "abstract,, words. i.e. those which have no concrete reference.

Compose a schematic sign designating each of these words. (this sign can be composed with the standard-stops)

These signs must be thought of as the letters of the new alphabet.

A grouping of several signs will determine

(utilize colors—in order to differentiate what would correspond in this [literature] to the substantive, verb, adverb declensions, conjugations etc.)

Necessity for ideal continuity. i.e.: each grouping will be connected with the other groupings by a strict meaning (a sort of grammar, no longer requiring
pedagogical
a sentence construction. But, apart from the differences of languages, and the "figures of speech" peculiar to each language—; weighs and measures some abstractions of substantives, of negatives, of relations of subject to verb etc, by means of standard-signs. (representing these new relations: conjugations, declensions, plural and singular, adjectivation inexpressible by the concrete alphabetic forms of languages living now and to come.).

This alphabet very probably is only suitable for the description of this picture.

Conditions of a language:
    The search for "prime
    words"
  ("divisible,, only
    by themselves and
    by unity).

3 Standard Stops =

_____ canned chance

1914.

the Idea of the Fabrication

horizontal
—— If a thread one meter long falls
straight
from a height of one meter on to a horizontal plane

twisting as it pleases and creates

a new image of the unit of length. ——

By perspective (or any other conventional

means . . .) the lines, the drawing are "<u>strained.</u>" and

<u>lose</u> the nearly of the "always possible,,

    with moreover the irony to have <u>chosen</u> the body or original
object which <u>inevitably becomes</u> according to this perspective
        (or other convention)

Breeding of Colors

— In the greenhouse
[On a glass plate, colors seen
transparently].

    Mixture of flowers of color i.e.

each color still in its optical state :

Perfumes$^{(?)}$of reds, of

blues of greens or of grays heightened

towards yellow blue red

or of weaker maroons. (the

whole in scales.). These perfumes

with physiological rebound can

be neglected and extracted in

an imprisonment for the fruit.

    Only, the fruit still has to

avoid being eaten. It's this

dryness of ''nuts and raisins,, that you

get in the ripe imputrescent

colors. (rarefied colors.).

— Regime of gravity —
Ministry of coincidences.
Department (or better):
Regime of Coincidence
Ministry of gravity.
Painting or Sculpture.
Flat container. in glass—[holding]
all sorts of liquids. Colored, pieces
of wood, of iron, chemical reactions.
Shake the container. and look
through it ——

Musical sculpture.
lasting and
Sounds leaving from

different places and

forming
sounding
a sculpture which lasts.

parts to look at
cross-eyed, like
a piece of silvered
glass, in which are
reflected the objects in the
room.

Rattle.

With a kind of comb, by
using the space between 2 teeth
as a unit, determine the
relations between the 2 ends
of the comb and some intermediary points
(by the broken teeth).

Use, as a
proportional control, this comb
with broken teeth, on another
object made up, also
of smaller elements
(smaller so that it can
accommodate this control. For
example: lead wires
more or less thick, laid
one against the other in
one plane (like hair).

Then, develop the
comb i.e. so that it
works abnormally
on a plane of lead
wires [or then turning
on a point, or even a
curved comb, i.e. not
flat or with teeth of unequal
lengths; or even the action of
these different models of
comb on a thick
material (lead wires) and
no longer just flat].
etc.

Sept. 1915

Classify
combs by the
number of their teeth

The Clock in profile.
and the Inspector of Space.

Razor blades which

cut well and

razor blades which no

longer cut

The first have

"cuttage" in reserve $\dfrac{\text{cutting}}{}$

—— Use this "cuttage"

or "cuttation"

The Bride stripped bare by her bachelors even.

to separate the mass-produced readymade from the
readyfound—The separation is an operation.

Specifications for "Readymades".

by planning for a moment

to come (on such a day, such

a date such a minute), "to inscribe

a readymade".— The readymade

can later

be looked for. (with all kinds of delays)
                              then
    The important thing is just

this matter of timing, this snapshot effect, like

a speech delivered on no matter
                    but
what occasion at such and such an hour.

It is a kind of rendezvous.

— Naturally inscribe that date,
                on the readymade
hour, minute, as information.

_____

    also the serial characteristic

        of the readymade.

Limit the no. of rdymades
yearly(?)

Make a
sick
picture
or a sick
Readymade

buy a
pair of ice-tongs
as a Rdymade

Readymade
Reciprocal=Use a
Rembrandt as an
ironing-board ——

Piggy Bank (or Canned Goods)
Make a readymade with
a box containing something
unrecognizable by its sound and
solder the box

---

already done in the semi Readymade
of copper plates
    and a ball of twine

: shadows cast by Readymades.

shadow cast by 2.3.4. Readymades. "brought together"

(Perhaps use an enlargement of that so as to

extract from it a figure formed by

an equal [length] (for example) taken in each Readymade

and becoming by the projection a part of the cast

shadow

       for example 10cm. in the first Rdymade   } each

             10cm.   —   2nd   —   } of these 10cm

                                   } having become

                etc.   } a part of

                                     } the cast shadow

Take these "having become" and from them make a tracing

without of course changing their position in relation to

each other in the original projection.

identifying

To lose the possibility of recognizing

2 similar objects —

        2 colors, 2 laces

2 hats, 2 forms whatsoever

to reach the Impossibility of
            visual
        sufficient memory,

to transfer

from one

        like object to another

the memory imprint

———— Same possibility

with sounds; with brain facts

Establish a society
in which the individual
has to pay for the air he breathes
(air meters; imprisonment
and rarefied air, in
case of non-payment
simple asphyxiation if
necessary (cut off the air)

on condition that (?)
Ordinary brick satiates the knot.
to be tired of

Note: The last three lines are not related to the foregoing statement, and the final line is
in English in the manuscript. GHH

Musical Erratum

This version of the Green Box is as accurate a
translation of the meaning and form of the original
notes as supervision by the author can make it.

Marcel Duchamp

New York 1960

APPENDICES

INSIDE *THE GREEN BOX*
George Heard Hamilton

DIAGRAM
Richard Hamilton

THE GREEN BOOK
Richard Hamilton

Our reasons for publishing an English translation of Marcel Duchamp's *Green Box* are not in the least mysterious. We would like the English reader to know and to enjoy one of the most complex as well as one of the most rewarding artistic experiences of modern times. And we thought that the best means of achieving this experience would be a typographic presentation which would preserve as much as possible of the visual appearance and effect of the facsimile manuscripts. In his own notes Richard Hamilton explains the problems which he faced and surmounted in achieving this edition. In these I wish only to mention a few of the implications of the manuscripts and of the work to which they refer.

That work is the large composition in oil paint, lead wire, and lead foil on two glass panels entitled 'La Mariée mise à nu par ses célibataires, même' ('The Bride Stripped Bare by Her Bachelors, Even'), more familiarly known as 'Le Grand Verre' or the 'Large Glass', or just the 'Bride'. Duchamp worked upon it in New York from 1915 to 1923 although it had been in his mind, as you will see, from as early as 1912. In 1923 he abandoned it, still unfinished. It was first owned by Walter Conrad Arensberg, the American poet and collector, who sold it to Miss Katherine S. Dreier when he moved to California in 1921, since he thought it too fragile to transport such a distance. His fears were justified. When it returned in 1926 from its first public appearance at the International Exhibition of Modern Art at the Brooklyn Museum, which Miss Dreier and Mr Duchamp had organized, it was smashed into a thousand pieces. Ten years later Duchamp repaired it, piecing the fragments together and securing them between two heavier panes of glass, the whole bound in a new metal frame. It was exhibited once more, at the Museum of Modern Art in 1943–44, before it joined the Arensberg Collection of Duchamp's works in the Philadelphia Museum of Art in 1953, by Miss Dreier's bequest.

Its seclusion accounts as much as anything else for the public's long reluctance to consider it as anything more than a joke, largely incomprehensible and not very funny at that. Nor when the *Green Box* appeared in 1934 did the documents, as precise in meaning as in form, do much to help. The intentionally random presentation encouraged one to think that there was no order of events in the 'Glass' itself. Duchamp's elegant invitation to the reader to thread his own way, with the aid of the notes, through the artist's mind went unattended by all except André Breton. In his searching and beautiful essay, 'La Phare de la Mariée', first published in *Minotaure* in 1935, he threw the light of his intelligence on the work by establishing the order of forms (we should really call them events) in the Bachelor's frustrated pursuit of the Bride. Although Breton's essay was twice reprinted (in *View* in 1945 and again in the Guggenheim Museum's catalogue of an exhibition of work by the three brothers Duchamp in 1957), it was little remarked. Nor did my own translation of twenty-five documents in 1954, as *From the Green Box*, mend matters for I avoided those which dealt with the 'Bride' and chose instead the peripheral 'jottings' (Duchamp's term), especially those for the 'readymades'. I then wrote that the 'Bride' is 'one of the inexplicable and inexplicably great works of art of our century'. And I argued that 'we begin to comprehend it, if not to understand it, when we realize that the solution is in itself insoluble'. Duchamp mocks me with the remark that 'there is no solution because there is no problem'. Meanwhile, in England and unknown to us, Richard Hamilton, using Breton's clues, had deciphered the bridal memoranda, put them in order, and in doing so discovered the relation of each note to the forms in the 'Glass', whether or not those forms were ever actually completed in the work as we know it. While we have been working on this edition, the English translation of Robert Lebel's *Marcel Duchamp* has been published, with his perceptive and poetic chapter on the 'Glass', and with Breton's essay once again. There is also now a French edition of Duchamp's collected writings, prepared by Michel Sanouillet under the title of *Marchand du Sel*. This includes the documents from the *Green Box* arranged in an order differing from ours. Thus the story of 'The Bride' is now available to all of us, and we can consider the significance of Duchamp's masterpiece and the activities related to it for the philosophy of modern art.

I use the word philosophy because for Duchamp art is a mental act, a fact of consciousness. His life, a long one, and his career as a professional artist, so disconcertingly short, have been dedicated to the deliberate annihilation of what he calls 'retinal painting', that sort of art which appeals principally or only to the eye, which he believes began with Courbet and reached its greatest splendors and deceptions in our times with Picasso and Matisse. What he wanted, we might say, was not a painting *of* something, but painting *as* something, painting which should not only represent an object but be in itself an idea, even as the object represented might not be actual in the phenomenal sense but rather a mental image. As he said in 1945: 'I wanted to get away from the physical aspect of painting . . . I was interested in ideas – not merely in visual products. I wanted to put painting once again at the service of the mind'. And again, in 1959: '. . . even though I tried in that big glass to find a completely personal and new expression, the final product was to be a wedding of mental and visual relations. In other words, the ideas in the glass are more important than the actual visual realization'. This statement confirms, if confirmation were required, our obligation to know by careful study the origins and development of the ideas set down in the *Green Box*.

So simply is his position stated; its consequences have been and still are incalculable. To Duchamp as much as to any one else we owe our present conviction that works of art are not imitations of the merely actual but are realities in themselves, and as realities they are not only objects within the physical world but objects of and in consciousness, 'brain facts' (*cervellités*, in his own word).

All this was less easily done than said. In the first place he had to call in question all traditional values, all systems of aesthetics, the whole history of art. If he did it with any one work it may have been with the second version of the 'Chocolate Grinder' of 1914, which appears for the third time as part of the principal male element in the lower portion of the 'Glass'. This was not so much a painting as a construction, since the milled sides and ends of the rotary forms were indicated by threads glued to the canvas and sewn to it at the intersections. In one sense, therefore, it was a *real thing*, not an illusion (as had been the earlier version in which spatial positions were conventionally indicated by modeling and cast shadows). The existence of the second version as a 'thing in itself' was further emphasized by the title and date stamped in gilt on a leather label and attached to the face of the canvas. Duchamp had abolished not only representational space but the concept of the picture as something precious and remote from our immediate existence. At the same time he had not created a 'real' machine; the 'Chocolate Grinder' functions only within the world of artistic decisions; its purpose is not physical but metaphysical, although what that purpose was took long to discover.

But the most important aspect of such objects as the 'Chocolate Grinder' remains to be mentioned: the interruption of the conventional collaboration between cause and effect, whether physical, psychical, or artistic. For the Cubists as for the Impressionists, the effect or the appearance of a painting was the result of its cause – the artist's experience of the original object, situation, or whatever had provoked the visual image which subsequently appeared on the canvas. Although the relation between object and image might seem less direct in a Cubist than in an Impressionist painting, the difference, as artists so unlike as Mondrian and Duchamp almost simultaneously observed, was relative rather than absolute. In the 'Chocolate Grinder' no such relation holds. Its source in anything so picturesque yet so banal as an actual machine observed in a chocolate manufacturer's shop in Rouen (which was the case), has been less forgotten than renounced. Duchamp's machine is not represented (re-presented), interpreted, or even transformed. It is a *different* machine, in kind as well as in intention. It is so different that it announces a new direction for both painting and machinery, which was soon achieved in the pictorially logical 'Glider' in the lower part of the 'Glass'. And now that the normal sequence of cause and effect had been obliterated, Duchamp was free to create such substitutes for art as well as for life. The danger of his position, its utter and daring originality, as well as his uncompromising and self-adjusting truth, lies in the fact that after almost fifty years the 'Bride' is still not a picture for most people, especially for those who confuse art with either life or nature when they try to justify one in terms of the other.

Our resistance to so plausible a position seems all the more curious when we accept or swallow whole, or even are indifferent to, far more startling proposals in other kinds of experience. Before these machines entered our world the non-Euclidian geometries and Einstein's theory of relativity had overthrown traditional concepts of space and time as measurable by the standards of common-sense. Duchamp admits that although such geometrical and physical theories were inadequately understood, they were topics of lively discussion before 1914. Since then we have seen matter not only dissolved into energy but even denied a fixed location in space, while space in turn has become more matter for philosophical speculation than for sensuous apprehension. But if Heisenberg's principle of uncertainty seems prophetically announced in Duchamp's notes, it would still be unnecessary as well as impertinent to look upon him as a prophet of scientific progress. A work of art, even of non- or anti-art, is never true or false from an extra-, non-, or anti-artistic point of view. But after all would it really be so strange if a current of cosmological speculation should achieve expression in two separate forms, pictorial and mathematic? Although Duchamp described his physics as 'playful', in the light of contemporary scientific thought they may not seem quite so amusing. They may be truer than we suspected to the nature of reality. His 'Glider', for instance, is made of a substance of 'oscillating density' (but are not all substances so?), and his 'Hook' has an indeterminate, variable, and uncontrollable weight (like everything else?).

Probably the most 'difficult' of Duchamp's concepts and creations are the 'readymades'. They are outrageous yet logical demonstrations of his suspension of the laws of artistic causality, for he has substituted for the traditional 'hand-made' work of art such ordinary, mass-produced, machine-made articles as a snow shovel, a comb, a bottle rack, or a bicycle wheel (set upside down on a kitchen stool). And the more commonplace they are the better since they make no appeal to the aesthetic of 'good design' or 'machine art', principles which were only defined long after he had made his decisions. The substitution of an anonymous article of everyday use for the conventional painting or sculpture can be understood only as an intellectual or philosophical decision. Wrenched from its everyday existence and denied every formal, technical, aesthetic, or even commercial value, the 'readymade' nevertheless exists and exerts its puzzling spell. It is simultaneously a visual demonstration, as Duchamp has said, 'of the futility of ever defining art', whether as process or example, and conclusive proof that all art, forever and everywhere, is ultimately only to be understood as a decision, as a mental fact, as the victory of consciousness over non-conscious matter, of will over taste.

The activity celebrated in the *Green Box* falls within the chronological limits of the Dada movement, which indeed was announced by Duchamp's activities in New York as early as 1915 and can be thought to have ended when he left the 'Bride' unfinished in 1923. The documents themselves are perhaps most easily deciphered if we approach them in the spirit of the deadly serious Dada jest. For is it not true that Dada objects, created in scorn and first greeted with disgust and ridicule, are now seen as desperately serious statements of our human all-too-human situations? In this spirit, and with a willing suspension of belief in any other world of physical or psychological law, these forms of thought will be comprehended as logical within the framework of Duchamp's speculations. They mean what they seem to mean, literally. And although the manner at times is obscure, it may help to remember that these are the verbal forms of the artist's thoughts set down as, when, and where they occurred. Some are carefully pondered, others are only fragments, glimpses of ideas emerging into consciousness, slivers struck from the mind like flashes of light from the shattered 'Bride'. Consequently the grammar is sometimes at fault, the syntax obscure, the sequence of ideas elliptical. We have tried to preserve all this in English so that you may share with us the pleasure we have had in trying to think through these thoughts and beyond.

At every stage in this process we have had Marcel Duchamp's generous support and encouragement. He has read and revised the translations three times, with scrupulous attention to the meaning and weight of every word. Our greatest satisfaction would be to think that the *Green Box* is now in English as he would have it.

George Heard Hamilton

New Haven, Connecticut, 1 May 1960

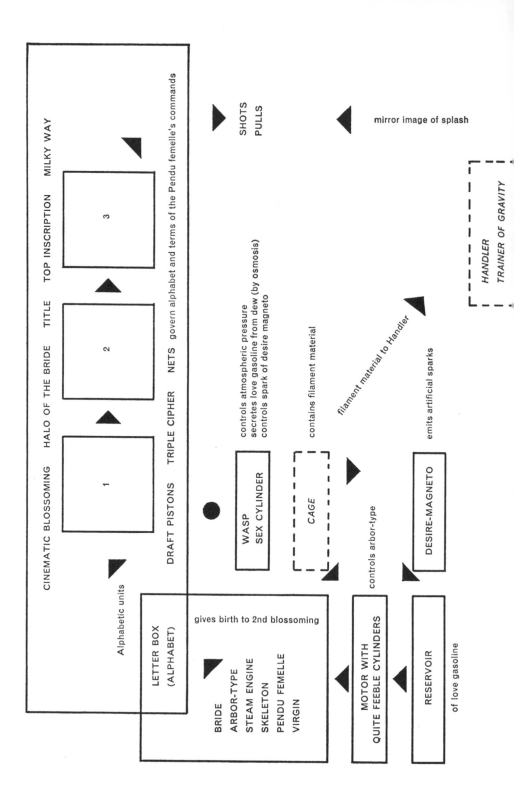

BRIDE MACHINE

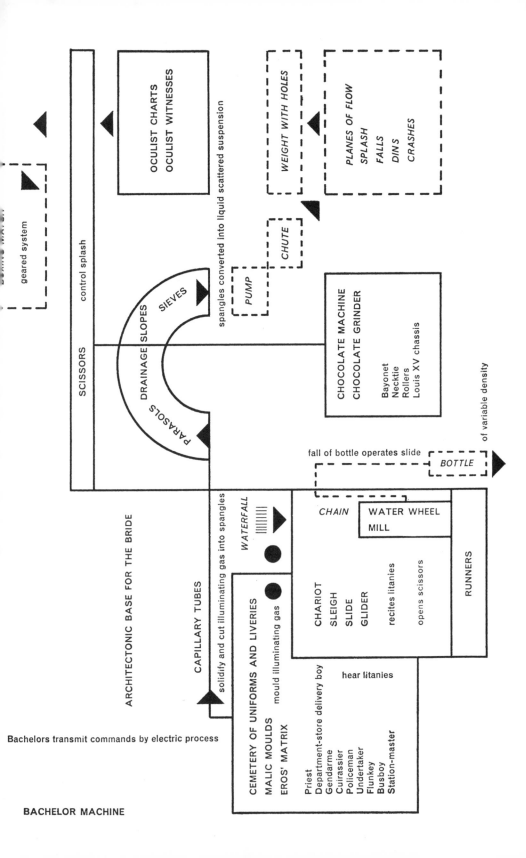

When Marcel Duchamp produced the work called 'The Bride Stripped Bare by Her Bachelors, Even' he contrived an art form without parallel, a unique marriage of visual and linguistic concepts. It was his intention that the 'Large Glass' should embody the realization of a written text which had assisted the generation of plastic ideas, and which also carried layers of meaning beyond the scope of pictorial expression. The text exists beside the glass as a commentary and within it as a literary component of its structure. Without the notes the painting loses some of its significance and without the monumental presence of the glass the notes have an air of random irrelevance.

Duchamp proposed to publish the writings so that his complete endeavour of the years 1912–23 should stand as a total work of art. But a period of eleven years passed before they were printed and then the documents emerged characteristically enigmatic – as a flat case containing ninety-four loose items; each handwritten note reproduced in exact facsimile including torn edges, blots, erasures and occasional illegibility: the Green Box, as it appears in the photograph on the flyleaf of this book, published by Rrose Sélavy in an edition of three hundred numbered copies in 1934.

No sooner has one begun to consider the advantages of a typeset version of the text than one appreciates the logic of Rrose Sélavy's decision to reproduce the notes in facsimile; for the actual meaning seems to suffer when calligraphy is converted to hard metal. This reaction is not the result of the strong affection that one inevitably feels for the hand of the artist – it is simply due to a realization of the impossibility of conveying the elaboration of information contained in the text by normal typographic means. What the facsimiles present, above all else, is the evidence of a prolonged meditation on art – a conscious probing of the limits of aesthetic creation. They convey the doubts, the rethinks and doubletakes, the flat bewilderment and the moments of assurance; the pauses and re-affirmations are there, the winces, private sniggers and nervous ticks. So loaded are these marks with the effort of their production that one soon sees that the permanence and clarity of type offer too overtly the arcane subtleties of Duchamp's thinking. A solution to the problem of a typographic rendering of the notes is to make a straightforward setting and then add a mass of footnotes to list the changes, insertions, stresses and other indi-cations less susceptible to treatment in type. This results in such a complex of references that it can only make more laborious a contact with ideas already difficult to reach. Given the possibility of editorial description of calligraphic oddities it remains impossible to project the sporadic nature of much of the writing which is often implied only by a change in the character of the hand itself or a change in the writing medium. To demand that such niceties of appreciation of the original documents should be communicated may seem pedantic to the point of fanaticism, yet that has been our aim in this book, for all the oddities of phrasing, punctuation, layout and typesetting are considered attempts to render as closely as possible the form of the original documents.

In the treatment of individual notes there was always a clear objective – the attainment of a direct equivalence between the facsimile and the typeset translation. But, of course, many factors intervene which make a complete analogy impossible. We tried to provide all the words and all the marks which convey the ideas and as much as possible of the variation of visual quality of the notes which gives clues to the way in which ideas developed and were modified. The one departure from this principle was in the treatment of erasures and obliterations – wherever there seemed to be a deliberate intention to make indecipherable a word, or group of words, it has been omitted but if a word or paragraph was crossed out but left clearly legible it has been so treated here. In our typeset version there is to be found a good deal of variation in the lengths of lines. This is due partly to the natural difference of line length determined by French and English grammar and spelling and partly to the removal of obliterated portions of the text. This uneven line length has given a poetic appearance to the page which should be regarded as a coincidental product of the principle of trying to match each line of French with a line of English. English grammar also made it necessary occasionally to transpose words from one line to another – this has been done with the minimum distortion of line values.

In general we have tried to maintain the individuality of the notes by giving each separate page of the original a separate page in the book. Here, again, departures from principle were necessary. The five text pages of the folded insert in this book consist, in the original, of a single sheet of paper concertina-folded to give ten closely written numbered pages. In a few cases two or more separate notes have been put on one page when the differences of type and position can adequately convey the distinctive character of each.

For the purposes of production in book form it was necessary to make decisions for which there was no model to guide the choice. Duchamp had no preference as to the order in which the notes appeared, so the sequence was determined by the typographer. Some of the documents are dated and some offer clues of chronology. Others are susceptible to grouping according to their theme or subject and within these groups the relationship of components to the major functions of the glass, and a progressive assurance in the author's grasp of a theme, suggested a suitable order. Three major factors were considered in establishing the sequence: (a) subject, (b) the relationship of the subject to the cycle of activity, (c) chronology and in that order of importance. For example, the Bride comes first because she seems to have reached a degree of completeness in her realization before the Bachelors have hardened into form, and the dating of certain pages confirms that precedence. On the other hand, the earliest document in the *Green Box* is a reproduction of the 'Coffee Mill', dated 1911, which doesn't appear in this book until quite late in the sequence; it is placed opposite a drawing which sketches an idea for a *butterfly pump* to appear under the last of the *cones* and prior to the *chute*. There are strong affinities between the form of the butterfly pump and the lower view of the grinder in the coffee mill, a connection which Duchamp himself would be loth to press, but since the 'Coffee Mill' marries less happily with previous material it is permitted to make contact if and when it can.

By 1914 most of the ideas had reached an advanced stage of elaboration and many of the components had been executed as separate studies. The extraordinary detailing of Duchamp's imagined subject, before he began work on the 'Large Glass', is revealed by the *plan* and *elevation* (1913) which show the elements of the lower part of the glass positioned to fine degrees of accuracy. This, almost physical, control of location in space is essential to the *trompe l'œil* treatment of these objects – a hallucinating effect of reality which can best be understood by an appreciation of the overall dimensions of the glass. It stands nearly nine feet high so that the junction, slightly above centre, between top and bottom comes roughly at eye level and coincides with the horizon at which the perspective is aimed. The perspective, so meticulously elaborated, manipulates human vision as consciously as a seventeenth century peepshow. The drawings which concern themselves with this organization of the perspective are like an engineer's plans in their disciplined execution. They have been redrawn for this edition. The decision to rework them was a calculated risk of restoration suggested by two needs. Three of them had become so smudged and dirty that all subsequent reproductions have borne less information than the original and the translation of words had to be substituted as inconspicuously as possible. The renewing process has used photographic techniques and a hand that has striven to remain as anonymous as that of a process engraver. Other drawings have received less reverent attention, but here also the departure from Duchamp's own hand can be justified by a claim to greater clarity in the transmitted signal and to a new unity between diagram and text which balances that of drawn note and handwritten description in the original. The sketches of components of the Bride are much more fluid than those of the Bachelors and depend for their quality on the Duchamp touch – so the Bride drawings keep his hand. As Duchamp informs in a telling note: 'The principal forms of the Bachelor Machine are imperfect: rectangle, circle, parallelepiped, symmetrical handle, demi-sphere=*i.e.* they are measurable'. The bachelor apparatus is so explicit that nothing is lost in making it more so. Most of the smaller sketches in the latter sections have therefore been remade with an increased precision.

Some twenty of the notes included in the *Green Box* do not deal directly with the subject matter of the 'Large Glass'. The anti-climax which occurs as a result of placing them together at the end of the book is accepted as an unavoidable consequence of my attempt to hold the continuity of the rest: the key to a full appreciation of Duchamp's masterpiece lies in an awareness of the sequential interrelationship of its component themes.

The notes describe the processes through which each element makes its contribution to the ultimate union of Bride and her Bachelors – the erotic climax of their activities. In the 'Large Glass' itself the function of apparatus can only be inferred from its construction. Some simple mechanical principles are not beyond the scope of pictorial expression: a drawing of an axle held free in bearings implies the possibility of rotation. But what picture can adequately convey the concept of love gasoline being distilled from dew? The *Green Box* informs at this non-pictorial level of experience. Water falls, the mill wheel begins to spin and starts the slow reciprocations of the chariot, we overhear its chanted litanies relieving the still silence of the cemetery of uniforms and liveries where the given gas is cast into malic forms. We become aware of the moulded gas seeping towards the elaborate conditioning which will prepare it for its final orgastic splashing and observe with wonder the beauty of its auras. The juices flow in the Bride, messages are transmitted from pools of random possibilities, the throbbing energy of a robotic world strains to create. *The Bride stripped bare by her Bachelors, even* rumbles into its fantastic splendour.

Richard Hamilton

London 1960